Always Remember, You are Loved

A Child's Curiosity about the Loss of a Loved One

Angel D. Washington

Illustrated by Curtis Perry

Book Designs by KG Media

Always Remember, You are Loved
A Child's Curiosity About the Loss of a Loved One

Copyright 2012 by Angel D. Washington

Illustrated by Curtis Perry
Book Designs by KGMedia

Published by Angel's Diary
www.angelsdiary1@aol.com

ISBN 978-0-986-00410-0

Author Photo by Destiny Washington

Acknowledgments

When parents teach their children humility, integrity and to live life with honor, love and respect, a child has the greatest potential to live the most fulfilling life that God has to offer. For these very lessons, I would like to thank my parents. I'm forever grateful for their love and support. I love you, Mama and Daddy.

To my sisters, April and Amber, we have what others wish for... I couldn't ask for better people to share my life's experiences. Wow, so many stories to tell, so little time! Love you.

To my brother, Ray, I pray that from HIS glorious, unlimited resources HE will empower you with inner strength through HIS spirit. Ephesians 3:16

To my sons, Christopher, KeyJon and Kyson, when the time comes and you are blessed with children of your own, be the best father(s) that you can be. Teach your children to love God, to be respectful, honorable and productive people. It will be your duty as parents to be supportive and involved physically, emotionally, and financially. Last but not least, love them with all of your heart, just as I love you.

To KH, throughout our journey, you have motivated and inspired me more than you know. Always Remember...

To my circle of friends, I thank you all for your unwavering friendship and support. I'm genuinely grateful for YOU, my FEW, yet TRUE and DEAR Sister Friends!

To our Heavenly Father, All Praises Be.

Angel D. Washington

Dear Reader,

When I wrote *Always Remember, You are Loved: A Child's Curiosity About the Absentee Parent*, many people hoped that the book also addressed the untimely loss of a beloved family member, close friend or companion. I vividly recall a woman whose young niece had lost her father in an automobile accident. The child's family was in search of the RIGHT words to say, the PERFECTLY CHOSEN words to explain such a tragedy to a young, curious and broken hearted child. At that very moment, I decided that *Always Remember, You are Loved: A Child's Curiosity About the **Loss of a Loved One*** would be written to assist each and every family that needed those carefully chosen words at the most emotional and difficult times.

As Parents, Guardians and Caregivers, we have a great responsibility to love and teach the children that we have been blessed with. There is no perfect way to explain the loss of a loved one. Yet, our children deserve our greatest efforts to ease their heartache and guide them in the direction of healing. It is my faith that this book will touch the heart of a child who is in pain. It is my dream that this book will provide healing and closure for those, children and adults alike, who have lost someone near and dear to their hearts and encourage them to treasure all of the wonderful memories left behind.

…And to ALL of those children out there, who have lost a loved one…

Always Remember, You are Loved.

Angel D. Washington,

A Mother, first & Author of the *Always Remember, You are Loved Series*

Dear Parents, Guardians and Caregivers,

It is a great honor to explain to children and model to them how to process major life events. I work for the Department of Family Services and have been a therapist trying to understand and heal wounded hearts for the past fifteen years.

One of the major life events that can wound a heart is the feeling of loss. The loss of someone that you love can feel devastating and hopeless. When the pain of loss comes into our lives it is an opportunity to model and explain the meaning of such a withdrawal. It is an opportunity to introduce Spirituality (Spirit) to a receptive and young heart.

When we are touched by someone's spirit and then their body dies what touched us continues to live on in our heart and spirit. It should also remind us of what we have <u>within us.</u> When we realize that we can share the same qualities that we admired in the person that passed …we are modeling that spirit does not die. Their spirit was here to show us and give us more of who we are. It reminds me of a song called, "More of Who We Are."

<blockquote>

"I will touch you with my soul.

Soul to soul let us touch again

And then may we behold more of who we are."
</blockquote>

Love never dies, so *Always Remember, You <u>are</u> <u>Loved</u>*.

Karmen Smith, MSW, LCSW, Ph.D, D.Div Child and Family Therapist, Ordained Minister

Always Remember, You are Loved

A Child's Curiosity about the Loss of a Loved One

Angel D. Washington

Illustrated by Curtis Perry

I don't understand why God took my Mommy away
I miss her and I want her with me everyday.
I wish my Mommy would come back
I need to hug her again.
I never even got to tell her that she was my
one and only best friend.
What do I do when I'm lonely and
my Mommy is gone?
Who do I go to when I need to question
what's right or what's wrong?
I need her, I love her, I miss her so much
I want to hug her, to kiss her... I need to feel Mommy's touch!

Your Mommy may not be here physically to share her love,
But she's here in spirit, she's watching from above
Please, Always Remember, You are Loved…
Always Remember, You are Loved

She loved you from the moment she held you in the fold of her arms
Your mother's strength and love will help you carry on
Your mother is an Angel in the Heavens above

Always Remember, You are Loved!

Just before bed, when the stars are bright,
Who will be here to laugh with me at night?
Who will I share everything with, from lip gloss to bows?
Who will tell me every secret that she knows?
I don't understand why God took my Sister away
What will life be like without her here everyday?
I love her so much, it's just not fair at all
When I get my first boyfriend in college, who will I call?

Your Sister may not be here physically to share her love
But she's here in spirit and she's watching from above
Please, Always Remember, You are Loved…
Always Remember, You are Loved

Your Sister will still be there to laugh with you at night
Just before bed, when the stars are bright
Your Sister loves you and smiles from above

Always Remember, You are Loved!

All of my friends have their Daddy's, but my Daddy is gone.
Is it because I misbehaved, did I do something wrong?
I promise that I will be good if my Daddy will come back
Or can I go away with him, will you help me pack?
Who will I turn to when things in my life don't feel complete?
Who will encourage me when my voice cracks as I begin to speak?
I beg YOU to give my Daddy back, I need him to be with me
God, don't YOU hear my prayers, do YOU see me on my knees?

Your Daddy may not be here physically to share his love.
He's your Guardian Angel sent from the Heavens above.
Please, Always Remember, You are Loved!
Always Remember, You are Loved…

Your Daddy didn't leave by choice, but he had to go
There was something that he wanted you to know
He loved you more than you could ever imagine
You were the love of his life, his baby, his passion

Please, Always Remember, You are Loved!
Always Remember, You are Loved ...

There was a grief counselor at my school today
That spoke to us because our classmate passed away.
There was one question that I didn't get to ask,
Does dying mean my classmate will never come back?

Your classmate went to a peaceful and serene place
But is with you every moment when you go out to play
Until your heart mends, I will be here to help you fix it
Whenever you need me, I'm here to talk or listen
On those days when you feel sad, it is okay to cry.
The pain and sorrow will ease with time.
Your classmate is playing in Heaven's
playground above.

Please, Always Remember, You are Loved!

I taught my little brother to play football, he was good too!
He would laugh and say, "*One day, I'll be better than you!*"
I would laugh and tell him that it's okay to dream
The day would never come, that he'd be better than me
For some reason God decided to take him away
Never again, will I see my little brother play
I love and miss him so much, what am I supposed to do?
I wonder if he really misses me too...

Always know that your brother is right by your side.
And will be every time you take your bike for a ride
He is one of God's Angels,that's why HE took him away.
He will be with you in every game that you play!
Your brother is MVP in God's Heaven above

Please, Always Remember, You are Loved!

Does my Grandma have her Angel wings now?
Did she travel to that place above the clouds?
Who will bake cakes with me and cookies, too
Who will babysit me, when I can't go with you?
I loved visiting you and Grandma during the summer
Do you think that she knew how much I loved her?
I need Grandma back, is she at Heaven's Gate?
I want her to come back now, please, can't Heaven wait?

I know that you miss your Grandma, but she's an Angel now
...and yes, she went to the place above the clouds
I also know that there are things that you don't understand
About Grandma's travel to the most peaceful land
Your Grandma may not be here physically to share her love
But she's here in spirit and she's watching from above

Please, Always Remember, You are Loved…

Always Remember, You are Loved!

Grandpa and I would have so much fun when I'd visit
Now he's gone and I will surely miss him
Can you please tell me why my Grandpa had to leave?
I'm just a kid and a Grandpa is what every kid needs
I tried to behave the best that I could
And I loved him as much as a grandchild should
I've lost him forever, my eyes hurt, all night I cried
I can't understand why my Grandpa died.

I am so sorry for your loss, I'm very sad, too
This is tough, but together, we will make it through
Whenever you need me, my Child, I'm here
… and no matter how far he seems, Grandpa is near
You brought so much joy to Grandpa's life, he loved you so
He loved you more than you will ever know
When you're feeling down, look to the sky, the Heavens above

…and Always Remember, You are Loved.

God took away my best friend and my friend was the best
Who am I supposed to talk to, laugh with and text?
Today is one of the worst days of my life.
My pillow will be tear soaked from crying all night.
To take away my best friend, what does it prove?
My friend is gone forever and why? I'm confused.
I wish God would come sit right here in my face
And tell me why HE took my best friend away.

Keep the memories of your friend close to your heart
And it will be like the two of you are never apart.
I know that the passing of your friend doesn't seem fair
Save the texts, cherish the memories and
the laughter you shared

With every moment of every day, your pain will improve
And whenever you need me, I will be here for you
Although your friend is gone to the Heavens above

Please, Always Remember, You are Loved!

My pet has been with me every day since the day I was born
Who will snuggle with me when I want to keep warm?
I don't understand why God would take my pet away
Is there someone in Heaven to walk my pet every day?
Who's going to wake me every morning before I go to school?
Who's going to make me laugh, but gross me out with drool?
This makes me very sad, I never want to have a pet again
There will never be another pet that can replace my furry friend

I'm certain that your furry friend will never be alone
There's a Pet Heaven that your furry friend can call home
With lots of space to run, play and go for long walks
Whenever you're sad, at any time, you and I can sit and talk
Pets are loyal, faithful and they make really good friends
One day your heart will heal and we can try again
Your furry friend is running and playing in Heaven's field above

Always Remember, You are Loved!

The End

Suggested Signs To Look For

In the unfortunate event of losing a loved one, children are often confused and will not know how to properly cope with their emotions. The following is a list comprised of emotional and behavioral ways that some children display or express during their grieving process:

Confusion/Denial
Declining behavioral/academic performance
Lack or inability to sleep
Lack or loss of appetite
Withdrawal
Sadness, Anger (Mood swings)
Regression in age appropriate behaviors
Nightmares
Fear (of death, abandonment, losing other loved ones)
Lack of interest in normal activities
Guilt

If the behaviors last for longer than two or three months (each child is different) and the child is not responding to loving attention by the caregiver, then grief counseling, grief camps or other interventions may need to be accessed. There may be a children's grief group in the community that may be available. Some interventions are found at the local hospice and of course the family church may be a good resource for helping a child grieve the loss of a loved one.

 "Healing begins within and then proceeds outwardly" ~ Karmen Smith, MSW, LCSW, Ph.D, D.Div

Always Remember, You are Loved Series
by Angel D. Washington

Always Remember, You are Loved:
A Child's Curiosity About the Absentee Parent

Always Remember, You are Loved:
A Child's Curiosity About the Loss of a Loved One

Always Remember, You are Loved:
When a Child Hides Emotional & Verbal Abuse in the Home

Always Remember, You are Loved:
When a Child Seeks Answers About Cyber/Peer Bullying

Always Remember, You are Loved:
Conversations with a Child about Inappropriate Touching

Email angelsdiary1@aol.com   Twitter @angelsdiary1 Angel's Diary on Facebook
Books available at www.angelsdiary.com or www.amazon.com or www.barnesandnoble.com

*All books in the Always Remember You are Loved Series are available or coming soon.

www.ingramcontent.com/pod-product-compliance
Lightning Source LLC
Chambersburg PA
CBHW041222040426

42443CB00002B/55